Desserts from Around the World

An Imprint of Pop!
popbooksonline.com

CUSTARDS
FROM AROUND THE WORLD

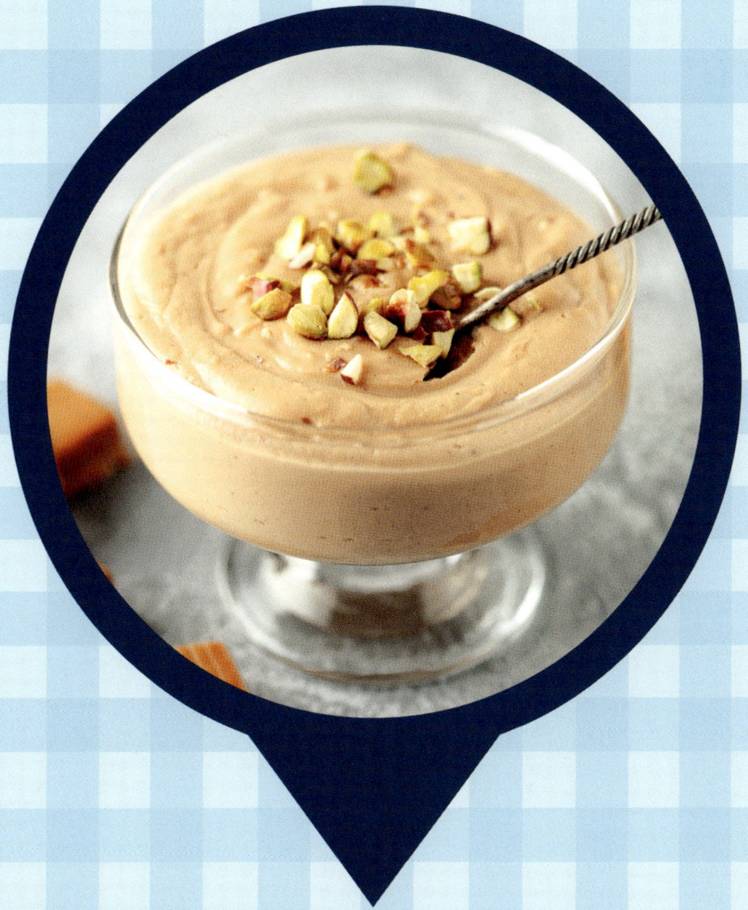

by Grace Hansen

WELCOME TO DiscoverRoo!

This book is filled with videos, puzzles, games, and more! Scan the QR codes* while you read, or visit the website below to make this book pop.

popbooksonline.com/custard

abdobooks.com

Published by Pop!, a division of ABDO, PO Box 398166, Minneapolis, Minnesota 55439. Copyright © 2025 by Abdo Consulting Group, Inc. International copyrights reserved in all countries. No part of this book may be reproduced in any form without written permission from the publisher. DiscoverRoo™ is a trademark and logo of Pop!.

Printed in the United States of America, North Mankato, Minnesota.
102024
012025

THIS BOOK CONTAINS RECYCLED MATERIALS

Cover Photo: Shutterstock Images
Interior Photos: Shutterstock Images, Getty Images
Editor: Elizabeth Andrews
Series Designer: Laura Graphenteen

Library of Congress Control Number: 2024938596

Publisher's Cataloging-in-Publication Data
Names: Hansen, Grace, author.
Title: Custards from around the world / by Grace Hansen
Description: Minneapolis, Minnesota : Pop!, 2025 | Series: Desserts from around the world | Includes online resources and index
Identifiers: ISBN 9781098247119 (lib. bdg.) | ISBN 9781098247676 (ebook)
Subjects: LCSH: Baking--Juvenile literature. | Desserts--Juvenile literature. | Baked products--Juvenile literature. | Cooking (Puddings)--Juvenile literature. | Confectionery--Juvenile literature. | Cookery--Juvenile literature.
Classification: DDC 641.864--dc23

*Scanning QR codes requires a web-enabled smart device with a QR code reader app and a camera.

TABLE OF CONTENTS

CHAPTER 1
The History of Dessert............ 4

CHAPTER 2
Custards from Europe 10

CHAPTER 3
Custards from the Americas 16

CHAPTER 4
Custards from Asia and Africa ... 20

More Custards from
Around the World! 28
Making Connections.............. 30
Glossary 31
Index & Online Resources 32

CHAPTER 1

THE HISTORY OF DESSERT

Desserts can be traced back to ancient times. The Mesopotamians had a fruitcake-like recipe. The Ancient Egyptians sweetened round, flat breads with dates and honey and cooked them over hot stones.

WATCH A VIDEO HERE!

Much of what we know about the Ancient Egyptians comes from wall paintings in temples and tombs.

The shape celebrated the sun and moon.

The Ancient Romans enjoyed simple sweet treats such as fruits, honey cakes, and fruit tarts.

This English oil painting from 1867 shows a first birthday celebration with cake and a candle.

In the 7th century, Persia (now Iran) was one of the first to harvest sugar cane and make cake-like cookies. In the 1500s, sugar became more affordable and widely available. In 1596, a cookbook was published for the growing middle classes in England. In it was a recipe for Fine Cakes. Later, Europeans made it more common to serve dessert, especially cake, for special occasions such as weddings.

Between 800 and 900, the Persians brought sugar cane to Southern Europe.

To this day, desserts help people around the world start the day, complete a meal, and celebrate important **milestones** and holidays. Let's go around the world and learn about custards from different places and **cultures**!

Almond cake, such as the one in this Ancient Roman mosaic, would have required a great amount of effort to prepare.

Mochi has long been enjoyed in Japan to celebrate the New Year. It was said to harden the teeth and therefore extend life.

CHAPTER 2

CUSTARDS FROM EUROPE

When people think of custard, the first thing that might come to mind is Crème Brûlèe! French for "burnt cream," Crème Brûlèe is known for its thin crust of caramelized sugar. The sugary shell is made using a **broiler** or kitchen blow

LEARN MORE HERE!

People love the combination of crunch and creaminess in Crème Brûlèe.

torch. A rich, delightful custard sits just below. Many countries, including France, Spain, and England, claim to be the birthplace of this special dessert.

Bavarian Cream is light and delicious.

Bavarian Cream is made up of a silky custard combined with **gelatin** and whipped cream. Traditional recipes call for it to be served cold and **garnished** with fresh fruit, crumbled cookies, or sweet sauces. Its origins are unclear. Some believe that French chefs working in Bavaria in the 1600s and 1700s learned the recipe then.

ENGLISH TRIFLE

Trifle is a layered dessert from England made of sponge cake or sponge fingers, fruit or jelly, custard, and whipped cream. Each ingredient is placed carefully in a clear bowl so that the lovely layers can be admired. Other recipes may include chocolate, coffee, or vanilla.

Vla is a traditional Dutch custard. In the Netherlands, there are rules when making true Vla. A **starch**, zetmeel, is one important ingredient. Vla must be made from at least 50% cow's milk. The milk's fat level must be at least 2.6%. The final product is a smooth, sweet, and delightful dessert.

Vla is relatively easy to make.

Vla is often sold in grocery stores. There are many Vla flavors to choose from, including caramel, chocolate, vanilla, coffee, and fruit.

CHAPTER 3
CUSTARDS FROM THE AMERICAS

Frozen Custard originated in Coney Island, New York. However, Milwaukee, Wisconsin, is fondly known as the "Custard Capital of the World." The thick frozen custard made with eggs, cream, and sugar is sold more

EXPLORE LINKS HERE!

(Top) Borden's Frozen Custard in Coney Island served 5 cent cones in the 1930s; (Bottom) Leon's Frozen Custard in Milwaukee opened its doors in 1942.

in Milwaukee than anywhere else in the world! Like ice cream and gelato, Frozen Custard comes in many flavors.

As the Roman empire expanded, so did recipes for flan.

While flan can be traced back to Ancient Rome, the Spaniards are credited with bringing the dessert to the Americas. Today, different versions of flan can be found throughout South America, Mexico,

DID YOU KNOW? Flan de Coco is especially popular in Colombia, Cuba, and the Dominican Republic.

and the Caribbean. One popular version is Flan de Coco. The recipe typically calls for simple ingredients, such as eggs, coconut milk, condensed milk, and vanilla extract. It is often baked in **ramekins** coated with tasty caramel. Before serving, the dessert is topped with delightful coconut flakes.

FILLED WITH CUSTARD

Many famous desserts are known for their custard fillings. France's Éclair is a **choux pastry** topped with chocolate and stuffed with custard. The Boston Cream Donut is a round, solid donut with chocolate frosting and a vanilla-flavored custard filling.

CHAPTER 4

CUSTARDS FROM ASIA AND AFRICA

Pumpkin Coconut Custard is a popular dessert in Southeast Asia. It is commonly found in markets and sold as street food in Cambodia, Thailand, and Laos. It is also served on special occasions such as the

COMPLETE AN ACTIVITY HERE!

Steam bakes the coconut custard inside of the kabocha or pumpkin.

Cambodian New Year. Coconut cream custard is baked inside a type of squash called *kabocha*. The finished product is a delicious and unique dessert. It is cut in slices to serve.

Dan Tat is a Hong Kong-style egg tart. It is a favorite dessert of the **Cantonese** people. Dan Tat is a combination of both British and Chinese tastes. In around 1920, the British introduced custard tarts to the city of Guangzhou. Over time, the Cantonese changed the recipe to

Derrick Yeung Siu-yep, director of Honolulu Coffee, holds a tray of the shop's signature egg tarts.

Dan Tat are perfectly sized for on-the-go eating.

reflect their tastes. The lightly-sweetened custard is commonly baked in either a shortcrust or puff pastry shell. Making the tart requires a lot of work, so it is not often done at home. But it is widely available in Chinese bakeries.

Melktert is often topped with a dusting of cinnamon.

DID YOU KNOW? South Africans celebrate National Milk Tart Day on February 27th.

Milk Tart, or *Melktert* in **Afrikaans**, is a creamy dessert that hails from South Africa. Like most custard-based desserts, Melktert finds its origins with Dutch settlers who **colonized** South Africa in the 17th century. The dessert consists of a sweet pastry crust and a custard filling.

Melktert can be served hot or cold.

Malva Pudding is likely the more popular South African dessert that includes custard. This dense and delectable baked pudding is made with apricot jam. A sweet, creamy sauce is poured over the pudding while it is still warm.

Many South African restaurants offer Malva Pudding.

Malva Pudding is traditionally served with custard, vanilla ice cream, or both!

MORE CUSTARDS FROM AROUND THE WORLD!

1. Butterscotch Pudding (USA)
2. Leche Poleada (El Salvador)
3. Pudim de Leite Condensado (Brazil)
4. Crema Catalana (Spain)
5. Canelés de Bordeaux (France)
6. Leche Flan (Philippines)
7. Vanilla Slice (Australia)

Countries and **cultures** around the world have their own unique and traditional desserts. Their ingredients and techniques can be similar to or very different from one another.

MAKING CONNECTIONS

TEXT-TO-SELF

Do you like custard desserts? If so, what is your favorite kind?

TEXT-TO-TEXT

Have you read any other books about food from around the world? What did you learn from those books that was not in this one?

TEXT-TO-WORLD

What are some other ways, besides dessert, that countries and cultures from around the world are special and different from one another?

GLOSSARY

Afrikaans — a South African language developed from seventeenth-century Dutch.

Cantonese — a native of the region of Guangzhou and Hong Kong.

choux pastry — very light pastry made with egg.

colonize — to establish a settlement on and begin to rule.

culture — the language, customs, ideas, and art of a particular group of people.

garnished — decorated with something that adds another flavor, color, or texture.

gelatin — an animal protein that is used for making things like jelly.

milestone — an important event or turning point in history or in a person's life.

ramekin — a small dish for baking and serving individual portions.

starch — a white tasteless powder found in many foods.

INDEX

Ancient Egyptians, 4–5
Ancient Romans, 5, 18

Bavaria, 13
Bavarian Cream, 13

Cambodia, 20–21
Caribbean, 19
Crème Brûlèe, 10–11

Dan Tat, 22

England, 7, 11, 13

flan, 18–19
France, 11
Frozen Custard, 16–17

Hong Kong, 22–23

Laos, 20

Malva Pudding, 26
Mesopotamians, 4
Mexico, 18
Milk Tart, 25
Milwaukee, Wisconsin, 16–17

Netherlands, The, 14
New York, 16

Persia, 7
Pumpkin Coconut Custard, 20

South Africa, 25–26
South America, 18
Spain, 11

Thailand, 20
Trifle, 13

Vla, 14

DiscoverRoo! ONLINE RESOURCES

This book is filled with videos, puzzles, games, and more! Scan the QR codes* while you read, or visit the website below to make this book pop.

popbooksonline.com/custard

*Scanning QR codes requires a web-enabled smart device with a QR code reader app and a camera.